ISBN 0-942044-03-7

Published by:
POLESTAR PUBLICATIONS
620 South Minnesota Avenue
Sioux Falls, SD 57104

Meeting Force With Silence

By

Dr. Terry Chitwood

POLESTAR PUBLICATIONS • Sioux Falls, South Dakota

ACKNOWLEDGMENTS

I want to thank my dog and two cats for not letting me out of the doghouse until I promised to write this book. I am grateful for the loving compassion I learned working with the men in my Arizona prison rehabilitation program. You showed me heart and courage with a childlike openness. Thank you. And finally, the most important thank you goes to my wife, Deb, who is a constant spiritual inspiration and who did the photography for the book without charging me.

CONTENTS

This book is dedicated
to nature for revealing
to me the secret
of her eternal teachings.

"In the stillness
    There is no sound
In the depths
    There is no motion"

—Deb Chitwood*

*From a collection of poems and forthcoming poetry book *Spring Sun, Spring Snow* by Deb Chitwood.

PROLOGUE

After receiving such a favorable response to my first book, *How To Defend Yourself Without Even Trying,* I thought that my readers would like another book written in a similar vein. However, writing a sequel was much more difficult than I had imagined. I have changed greatly in the three years that it took me to complete this book. Some of the changes may be evident in my writing, some not. Perhaps, unless you write fiction, you can only write about where you have been rather than where you are now or where you are going.

I hope that *Meeting Force With Silence* will touch people as deeply as *How To Defend Yourself Without Even Trying* has done. As Bob Dylan once lyrically said, "The times they are a changing." That is certainly true of the 1980s. Today's pace is so accelerated that many people lose the sense of their own center, the sense of their own soul. If by reading this book, you feel closer to your own essence, your own uniqueness, then I have accomplished my purpose. Enjoy the book, and remember that the most important path in life is the individual path, not the group path.

"The universe has a great sense of humor."

Reflections

THE MEN'S ROOM

While attending a dance during my adolescence, I decided to go to the men's room. After entering the room, I rapidly procured a urinal. Two urinals to my right was a large fellow with a reputation for being mean and tough. I became aware of his presence but remained unafraid. I turned, walked out of the men's room, and thought nothing of it.

Much to my surprise, a friend excitedly pulled me to the side. He asked me if I was aware of what happened in the men's room. I said, "Outside of the usual goings on, no." Then my friend described a fascinating incident.

He explained that as I turned to walk out of the men's room, the mean fellow curled back his fist and took a full swing at my head. It looked like a ballet, since I was moving forward just enough to avoid the swing. The mean fellow missed. Everyone who saw it was amazed. So was I, by the universe's gift of protection.

KARATE COMEDY

When I was in the armed forces and stationed on Guam, the local toughs had a reputation for trouncing American servicemen. They would beat Americans with pipes and clubs, or they would stick a wooden plank out the window of a moving car and whack a walking American.

One day on an isolated surfing beach, two friends and I were enjoying the sun and sea. As we surfed, a car full of islanders pulled up next to my car. The driver stepped out and boldly walked over to look at the contents of my car through its windows. He then proceeded to sit on my car's hood. Now when anyone proceeds to invade even your car's territorial space with such abandon, it means trouble. However, since it was fifteen miles back to the base and the car was our only transportation, we had little choice in our actions.

As we approached the beach, the man on my car hood started walking toward the water. We walked past him with no problems. Previously, I had taken the back seat out of my '57 Ford to make room for our surfboards. As I was placing our boards into the car through the trunk, I saw movement out of my left peripheral vision. Then I felt a pain in my jaw as a fist connected full force with it. I spun off the car to see another man attacking my two friends with kicks and punches and yelling, "Karate, karate!" I thought, "What a strange thing to yell at a time like this."

Little did I know that his words had a special meaning for me. I started taking karate within the next month. It was as if the universe moved through him (disturbed as he was) and told me to take karate lessons. Previous to this encounter I had only studied judo. Back to the story.

After spinning off the car and seeing my friends attacked by the crazy man yelling "Karate," I was approached cautiously by a man making jerky karate movements. Before I had time to contemplate this theatre of the absurd, there were six men against three of us. Since I could count to six, I rapidly thought and proceeded to yell, "Down to the water!" We three ran down to the ocean's edge. I felt safer knowing I could handle myself against many opponents in the water. My two friends were down the beach a few hundred yards from me.

Three men made a semicircle in front of me (I faced the land) and took karate stances. I did what came instinctively and picked up a large (but harmless) bamboo log and tossed it at them with a yell. Naturally, I missed. The log was too big to hit anyone with, and I did not really want to hurt them. Then the three men standing only ten feet in front of me began throwing rocks and taunting my friends who were hundreds of yards away. In the meantime, the other men were trying to find possessions to steal from my car. Ultimately, they got a few worthless objects.

Just as this whole absurd drama was unfolding, a Guamanian police car was coming down the hill (this was the first and last police car I ever saw in this isolated area). Our assailants spotted the police car, ran excitedly toward their car, and sped off. We flagged down the police car and began our merry chase. Naturally, we did not catch our assailants because even most Guamanian policemen resent Americans.

That was my first experience with karate comedy. The attackers were good enough to bloody my lip when hitting me from behind, but that was about it. I am not saying that the incident was without danger. Many islanders carry knives and other weapons. Although our attackers did not display any weapons, they may have been carrying them. So that was my introduction to karate (probably just so I could write this entertaining tale). The universe has a great sense of humor.

PARTY KICKS

One late night at a party during my college days, a man who had one drink too many approached me. He was in a disagreeable mood and proceeded to be insulting. Since I had been studying karate intensely for the last three years, I felt I would have an unfair advantage if the drunk provoked the altercation into physical violence.

I attempted to explain to the drunk that he really did not want to fight me because I was well-versed in the art of karate. I repeatedly tried verbally to avoid a fight. Finally, since he did not appear to understand what I was saying, I placed three rapid front kicks just below the tip of his nose (not touching him). Even in his inebriated condition, actions seemed to speak louder than words. The drunk proceeded to slink away in embarrassment. He had three kicks too many.

SYMBOLS OF POWER

During my junior year of college, I resided in the men's dormitory for one semester. That semester proved both interesting and enlightening.

There were two groups of people on our floor: the football players and the intellectuals. The football players threw wild parties where both furniture and people would get broken. The intellectuals were intimidated by the athletes' physical prowess and wild rampages.

Since I was known to be proficient in karate, I was asked to show how good I was one evening by an almost seven-foot tackle. His friends were gathered around watching. I decided to demonstrate the essence of sanchin, a karate kata which produces a zen state of mind if done correctly. I took the basic stance, began the sanchin breathing, and told the tackle to hit me full force in the abdomen. He wound up, swung, and his punch bounced off like rubber. He punched me twice more before he could believe his eyes. The quiet in the room after the incident showed silent respect.

The point of this story is that thereafter my presence had a symbolic effect. One night a group of football players had surrounded a long-haired activist and were hassling him. As I stepped out of the elevator, the scene unfolded. I watched the provocative behavior escalate until one athlete spit on the activist's hair. The radical remained calm. I walked behind the outnumbered man and stood quietly. The athletes looked at each other and then quietly dispersed. This incident illustrates the power of the symbol. In the athletes' minds, I was symbolic of great power and force. Their mental image of me made them disperse, not my physical presence. In fact, had the situation resorted to physical force, I may have very well been defeated. I was outnumbered by large, strong men and had a small space in which to maneuver.

The lesson is to cultivate calmness, confidence, and centeredness. These qualities can quietly disperse a dangerous situation by acting as symbols of power. Once a situation comes to blows, anyone can win.

FRIENDLY TOUGHS

One evening when I was young and adventurous, a friend, his dog, and I were hitchhiking through Iowa. At that point in our lives, all three of us had fairly long hair. Since we were hitchhiking on the main street in a small town, the local boys thought it would be fun to taunt us. The taunting was slight at first. I thought it best to avoid trouble by exiting the main street and attempting to find a ride on the highway by the edge of town.

After reaching the outskirts of town, it became dusk and rides were scarce. Just then, three carloads of the locals pulled up in a vacant lot about fifty yards from us. In an intuitive flash, I realized that unless we acted immediately we would be in serious trouble.

So with a buoyant stride and a happy demeanor, I walked over to the first car, knocked on the side window, and motioned for the occupants to roll the window down. Down the window came. I stuck my head part way into the car and said, "How are you doing? It looks like a good night for a drive." They all seemed to be disarmed by my unfearful and sincere behavior. We talked briefly and congenially. Then the first car left, followed by the other two. Approaching fear with love can save the day—even in real life.

THE BROKEN ARM

One day during my work with my Arizona prison rehabilitation program, I was teaching aikido to a student in a matted area within the prison dormitory. Another convict walking by the room looked in and said, "That stuff does not really work." I said, "Come in and give it a try." Skeptically, he walked into the room. I said, "Hit me as hard as you can." He took a full-force swing, and I blocked it effortlessly. I asked him if he would like to try again. He said, "No," sheepishly.

Later, the student I was working out with told me that the convict whose punch I had blocked went back into the dorm and told the rest of the prisoners, "That Chitwood's a bad dude. I threw a punch at him and his block almost broke my .*!@ arm." I appeared to earn his respect.

The moral of this story is that sometimes people do not believe words or anything but their own experience. These people will only understand a physical display of power. It is best to keep the display to a minimum. The convict's arm was hurt by the force of his own punch. My arm was not even sore. In essence, he hurt himself. If a situation would come to blows, most likely the assailant of an aikido practitioner would only hurt himself through his own aggression.

Regrettably, it may occasionally be necessary to physically defend yourself against certain hard-headed individuals. When avoiding dangerous places or using gentle words does not work, you may be required to run away or physically defend yourself. Do so with the strength of your spirit.

EVERYONE NEEDS LOVE

One day I was conducting a group session in my prison program in Arizona. I was using self-mastery techniques to tear down the convicts' games and acts. Their acts or false images prevented them from seeing their true inner selves.

I said something that offended one man who happened to have a bad temper. He ran up to my face, stared at me, and yelled that he was going to kill me. Now some of these fellows in my program had murdered people. However, I used my intuition to sense if there was any true danger. I did not feel that he would hurt me. So I said just that: "Rick, I do not think that you want to hurt me. You know I care about you." This statement totally disarmed the situation and allowed the previously out-of-control convict to discuss the matter more rationally.

This incident illustrates the importance of intuitively sizing up a dangerous situation before acting. Then act on your intuition. Your actions should prove correct.

NIGHT PICNIC

One night my wife, Deb, and I were walking through a park in a city. A man sitting on a picnic table in a dark area to our left said forcefully, "Come over here." Instead, sensing danger, I concentrated my mind and intention while continuing to walk straight ahead. Within two seconds, the man said, "I'm sorry, sir. Have a good night." I replied, "I hope you, too, have a good night." This incident illustrates that single-pointedness of mind can telepathically disarm a potentially dangerous situation.

BLEND INTO A TREE

One night in a city, Deb and I were walking toward a park. I sensed danger from behind, and a carload of suspicious-looking fellows in an old rattletrap of an automobile rode by and yelled obscene remarks. Of course, since there was no way to avoid their remarks, we did the next best thing. We ignored them.

I knew the men would return, so I told Deb to walk faster in order to reach the park. Sure enough, once we reached the park, the car came around the block and the men were looking for us. I told Deb to blend into a tree. We both picked a tree and leaned close against it. The car had stopped about one-half block away, and the men were visually searching the area for us. However, we were not to be seen. We had blended into the natural surroundings and avoided a potentially harmful situation. The car raced away.

". . . let go of ideas that cannot laugh."

Perceptions

". . . through your spirit you realize the eternity in all things."

PASSAGES

As you pass through the birth canal and out into the light, time seems to stand still. Each breath takes forever.

As a child, days linger and you savor their individual flavor. Leaves fall slowly from the trees and the seasons seem to last forever.

Adolescence brings love and passion—an eternal spring. New emotions toss you about like the restless sea does the small wooden boat. Change precedes change.

Early adulthood brings challenge. Blood flowing restlessly through your veins, you test your skills, your courage. No mountain is too steep to climb. No cave is too dark to enter. Perpetual energy has its way with you.

Middle adulthood leaves you gasping. How did you get here from where you started? All the paths not taken are vividly seen. All the paths that cannot be taken are contemplated and gently discarded. Life is accelerating and years seem like months. Time has changed its color.

Late adulthood brings a mellow acceptance. You have seen more suffering than you had ever cared to see. You have experienced more joy than you had ever thought possible. You have seen friends die, babies born. Your body is different, but your spirit is the same. And through your spirit you realize the eternity in all things. They change and yet remain the same. Seasons come and go. The rain falls and the sun rises.

"Each moment has important signs willing to aid you in your life's path."

DREAMS

Dreams are your friends. They are your guides through the struggle of life. When you need help, they give it. When you are lost and confused, they show you a way out.

In order to listen to your dream guidance, you need to know the language. Dreams speak in symbols and images. Instead of interpreting the symbols, let them speak to you. Let them reveal their meaning through dialogue. If you want to know what a symbol means, befriend it and ask it. Until you truly love your symbols, they may be hesitant to reveal their total meaning and importance.

Life is like a dream. People, events, and situations can speak to you, if you let them. Each moment has important signs willing to aid you in your life's path.

Just as symbols occur in dreams, so they occur in external reality. And, until you understand their messages, they are going to repeat themselves. Until your patterns are clarified, they cannot be dissolved.

Life is truly magical. Birds can help you find your direction, rocks can speak, and rivers can sing.

Only if you close your heart to life, does life lose its magic.

External symbols and dreams release energy for constructive purposes. Flowing is being in tune with your individual symbols. Happiness is living in harmony with your dreams. Using your new-found energy for bringing joy to all living things can only help bring peace that much closer to reality.

". . . every situation, person, and event that comes your way in life is meaningful to your spiritual growth."

MIRACLES

Miracles can happen if you let yourself be. Struggling on behalf of an idea can make you a slave to that idea. Holding on too tightly restricts not only your blood flow but your life flow as well.

Miracles need space in which to happen. If you empty your mind of the way things ought to be, then you are creating space for the universe to do its work. If people or situations are not responding according to your conscious plan, realize that they are there to give you direction. Once you take the direction, miracles can happen.

Did you consciously navigate the birth canal? Yet here you are. I am not saying that you should strive for total unconsciousness. You could do that by hitting yourself on the head with a baseball bat. What I am saying is that every situation, person, and event that comes your way in life is meaningful to your spiritual growth. By discerning the meaning of an event, you create the proper environment in which miracles can occur.

Allowing miracles to happen is probably the hardest and simultaneously easiest thing that you can do. The mental climate in which they occur requires that you not anticipate, plan, or expect what specifically will occur. Giving up conscious direction allows the universe to act freely. Perfect situations occur more readily when you do not expect them. It is also more exciting when they do occur. Surprise is more fun than precise prediction.

So do not waste your energy with control games. Let go of your vision of life, and let life embrace you. Move slowly and gently toward the future. Give miracles the freedom to happen spontaneously—and with great delight.

" . . . many of your meetings
with significant people in your
life had a magic to them."

MAGIC

Many people go through life stuck in a rut. They think that digging their rut deeper is making progress. If you ask them for assistance, they will give you a preprogrammed response that will be an affront to your individuality.

To avoid ending up like these people, you need intelligence, curiosity, motivation, and magic. Magic is the energy that captures your attention with its effortless results. Magic is being in the right place at the right time—consistently.

Remember your first meeting with a significant person in your life—possibly your husband, wife, or a good friend. Did events seem to work to make your meeting inevitable and effortless—possibly even exciting and surprising in its unexpectedness? I am sure that many of your meetings with significant people in your life had a magic to them. The meetings seemed preordained.

It is important to trust life's magic during difficult periods in your life. Let go of the people, possessions, and concepts that are no longer needed. This creates an emptiness where magic can be manifested. Spontaneous events and newness can happen more readily in an uncluttered life.

If you look around at your life and do not see much magic in it, perhaps you do not want things to go easily. Many people are so secure in hardship that it would be like leaving an old friend were they to give it up. Of course, this does not apply to you. You probably think you are too aware, too smart, or too something for this to be a description of you. However, if your life is a drudgery and the magic is not there, then take a cold and harsh look at yourself. No doubt you like things as they are—for whatever reasons.

Magic and excuses do not mix well. If your head is full of excuses for why your life is the way it is, then magic will be far away. Drop your excuses and seek magic as a friend.

Certain people even hate magic. They despise perfection. Their slogan is "Nobody's perfect." Translated, this can mean "Do not try to do anything well." If you do make an attempt to do something perfect and make a mistake, they will be there to club you with "Nobody's perfect." However, this is looking at the small picture. In the big picture, mistakes are perfect. If properly understood, they provide the direction you need to take in order to be more fully yourself. They can even be fun and exciting—and make you laugh. A mistake could even save your life. For instance, while driving a car you could make a wrong turn but avoid a fatal crash.

Magic befriends people who are not afraid of making mistakes. If you want joy, laughter, and magic in your life, then stop being so fearful. Be bold and pursue your destiny enthusiastically. That way, magic is sure to be your companion.

"Desiring something that is not in your life's path could cause you unnecessary hardship."

FALSE HOPE

False hope can keep you locked into a course of action that is no longer bearing fruit. You may persist at tasks that are seemingly important only to later realize that you have just been stubborn. The tasks were worthwhile only to your conscious, egocentric plan.

False hope is the motivator of incorrect action. Incorrect in the sense that it does not lead you toward your life's work. Wanting to be rich when you are not meant to be could be an example. If your life's work were to live and work among the poor, wealth could possibly be a detriment to your destiny—even only if it made you feel superior.

Desiring something that is not in your life's path could cause you unnecessary hardship. You could stumble around with dead ends for many years before being led into your correct life's path. It is important to learn how to recognize the dead ends and the false paths.

What if your life's work is only to be an exceptional parent? Would your ego scream at you because you should be something greater—by its definition, of course. Or what if you love carpentry, but you finished college and there is pressure from relatives and friends to pursue a career based on your college training? Would you have the courage to choose your own way—however simple or unimpressive it may seem?

These are not easy questions, nor are they meant to be. Many varieties of false hope originate because of your desire to please family and friends. One common unconscious assumption would be, "If I just do this (what they want), then they will love me." Some hardheaded people can choose the wrong work for a lifetime based on the previous assumption or a variation thereof. But you do not necessarily want to rebel against the wishes of your family and friends, either. Do not choose another path based on the unconscious premise, "If they want me to do it, it has to be wrong. I will do the opposite or anything but this (what they want)." What if what they want happens to be your life's work? Some people can rebel for a lifetime, also.

How can you distinguish between false hope and your real work? Actions carried out based on false hope will receive a series of obstacles that will discourage you from continuing in your direction. Sometimes it is difficult to distinguish between obstacles and tests, but it can be done. Tests usually lead to understanding and growth whereas obstacles lead to frustration. The frustration's purpose is to get you back on the right track.

False hope also causes a hardness and impatience. Your true path should feel natural and soft, even with the tests.

So stop chasing what you do not want. Let go of what you do not enjoy. Travel light and easy. You have been designed specially to fulfill your unique place in life. Why should not your life's work be a joy?

"You attempt to steer your life in one direction, and events shove you in another."

CONTROL

Control is a complex concept. You have less control than you think. Your heart pumps your blood without your conscious decision and your dreams come unbidden.

Have you ever tried to establish a relationship with someone who was incompatible with you? No matter how hard you tried, the separation remained. The relationship lacked a certain spark, an essential ingredient. You could not control its outcome.

So it is with much of life. You cannot control its outcome. You attempt to steer your life in one direction, and events shove you in another. Sometimes, it appears like you are the ball in a cosmic tennis match—it is difficult to see which side of the court you are on, much less stop for a rest.

If life is such a roller-coaster ride, why plan for anything? Because planning is part of the ride. Planning sets you in motion. And motion is what helps you progress to your next lesson in life. Make flexible plans, subject to the intervention of the universal will.

Let life move you. Allow situations to unfold naturally without your conscious interference. If a friend wants to leave, share your feelings and let him go. If you lose your job, see the perfection in the loss. Make the move to a more enjoyable position that will further your growth. There is an underlying reason for everything, even if you cannot presently piece things together.

Rather than using control, use your intuition to allow your spirit to guide you. Let your feelings attract you to the right decision—the right life move. Relax and allow life to unfold according to the universal plan.

"When you spread your opinions where they are not wanted, you are interfering."

NONINTERFERENCE

Having an opinion to fit every situation may make you seem intelligent, but only to yourself. Life is not so simple. It is incredibly complex. Having all the answers makes you rigid and old, not smart.

Opinions make you feel safe, even if they are untrue. As long as you think you know the truth about a subject, you feel secure. It is an illusory security, requiring a constant defense against other input. The truth does not need a defense.

When you spread your opinions where they are not wanted, you are interfering. You are forcing your way into the mind of another. Unwanted opinions are like verbal clubs. They hurt the person receiving them.

If you want to make people tense, angry, or sad, try pushing your opinions on them. Find the right button and use an opinion to push it. You will not make a friend, but were you trying to?

That is why noninterference is a concept that works. If you let situations unfold naturally and share your views when appropriate, then everything will progress smoothly. Your relationships will improve and your head will feel lighter. Breathe the peace of noninterference. You cannot be truly happy without it.

"If you lack humility, your life will be plagued by suffering."

HUMILITY

Humility is a necessity, not a virtue. It is a gift rather than a role. If you lack humility, your life will be plagued by suffering. This is because your ego will have to be corrected by the direct intervention of the universe through harsh tests—better known as reality.

An ego's nature is to raise itself up. The universe's nature is to make sure your ego falls—abruptly and without warning. Your life will feel like it has been ripped apart, torn in a dozen different directions at once. You will think that an earthquake picked your mind to rest in. Your body will shiver and your heart will desire forgiveness.

This is why humility is a necessity. Who in their right mind would want to bring these trials upon themselves? Most everyone you know, including yourself. No, you do not do it intentionally or consciously, but you do it nevertheless. You set yourself up to get smashed.

Why do you indulge in your own self-centeredness? Why is your concern for your will and desires first and foremost? Maybe you like pain. Because pain is inherent in those attitudes.

Adopt an ego-filled attitude and pain will be forthcoming. With an ego-filled person, reality will eventually intervene to maintain a proper balance. Of course, initially reality may have to swing harshly in one direction to correct the enormity of the error.

Although the picture I have painted seems rather harsh, it is not. It is a blunt description of the way things are. Observe others, your friends, and yourself for a prolonged period of time. You cannot help but notice that my description is correct, perhaps an understatement.

Make humility your friend. With humility around, you stand less of a chance of self-induced pain. If you are fortunate, you have already been gifted with humility. Treasure this gift. However, do not pretend to be humble. That is probably one of the most ego-filled things you could do.

"Everyone needs to tell his story."

FREEDOM

Freedom is an elusive concept—the closer you come to understanding it, the more it moves out of your grasp. What place does it have on a planet where all creatures and all things are connected? Surely that is a question to begin with.

Perhaps, you feel much pain in your life. Let us say that you undertake a therapy that promises you freedom from this pain if only you work through your childhood and birth traumas. Disregarding the fact that this "working through" could take you more than one lifetime, let us say that you begin the process.

One day, if you are perceptive and honest with yourself, you will start wondering why there still appears to be an endless well of pain to work through when you have been working on these emotions for years. In fact, the well now seems deeper and wider. Also, curiously enough, your trauma seems boring at times and you are really not that screwed up anymore.

What is happening here? What is happening is that you have cleared out your personal suffering enough to tune into the seemingly endless suffering of the human race. As the saying goes, "I will not allow myself to enter total enlightenment until all others have gone before me." Well, you may not have much choice. Sure, you can isolate yourself from people, keep your meditation at a certain level (peace, bliss, whatever), but a gnawing feeling will keep whispering in your ear: "What about the suffering? What about the suffering?"

Enter compassion. If you have not lost your heart on the spiritual path, then you will reach out to people with your spirit and understand them. Everyone needs to tell his story. Open your heart and listen. Freedom may yet find a space to enter.

". . . you should be aware of the people who populate your day."

FLAKES

When I speak of flakes I am not speaking of snowflakes. I am speaking of people who do not do what they agree to do. They are the time wasters, the energy drainers.

Hey, Terry, I thought you were a positive, rambling kind of guy. What is it with all this harshness? The ocean waves are impersonal. They roll over good and bad swimmers alike. However, the poor swimmer may drown, and the good swimmer could survive. The environment impinges upon people like the ocean waves. Some days are stormy, some sunny. Some days are frantic, some relaxed.

The point I am making is that you should be aware of the people who populate your day. They can cause an otherwise sunny day to cloud over with great rapidity—or make a cloudy day sunny.

Now flakes do not usually walk in through your door and say, "Hi, I am a flake. I am here to waste your time and suck your energy. All you have to do is sit back and develop a headache, stomachache, or your favorite symptom while I do my routine." What a kinder world that would be.

However, expert flakes are usually subtle. You

have to look closely to discover their furtive manipulations. One way to identify them is to examine the use of your time spent with people. Was the time spent useful, enjoyable, necessary? Or did it seem to evaporate, drag, or disappear with nothing accomplished?

Life is too short to waste your time being with people who make you sick. Develop the courage to rid your life of its flaky clutter.

". . . you may want to dig deep into yourself and find your buried treasures."

QUALITY OF FEELING

You can go through life pretending that you are never angry, anxious, or sad, but then you lose the ability to truly feel. Unfortunately, many people have a phony calm demeanor and speak profusely about how loving they are. This is particularly true with people associated with the new-age movement. However, the aggression of these individuals manifests itself when they invade your space with an unwanted hug. Or, perhaps they cheerfully chastise you for your saying something real rather than something positive.

The point is that if you want to be part of the new age or any other group that espouses conformity of behavior, thought, and speech, you may lose your soul. So instead of trying to function on a higher plane of existence, you may want to dig deep into yourself and find your buried treasures. These treasures may be surrounded by guardian feelings such as hate that have turned uglier over the years because they have remained unrecognized. However, underneath your hate, anger, and sadness lies the possibility of true inner unity and peace. Rather than avoiding feeling your pain by engaging in certain "spiritual practices," welcome your pain as a friend who is guiding you home.

When over the years you consistently and repeatedly face your pain, you will be rewarded by a feeling of solidity or a renewed inner exuberance. This new zest for life is what I refer to as quality of feeling. Until you experience it on a consistent basis, you will not realize what you have been missing. So instead of running away from your quality of feeling by pursuing a shallow search for enlightenment, drop the false and unreal beliefs from your repertoire and experience your own truth.

Remember that quality of feeling is not your birthright to be given to you instantly by pursuing the latest therapy or spiritual fad at a weekend workshop. It is the result of years of sincere effort in confronting the pain of your existence. There is no shortcut on the path of truth, and only your personal integrity will guide you in the right direction.

"The mystery of life exists in its paradoxes . . . . "

ILLUSIONS

Every now and then you will meet someone who thinks he has all the answers. If only life could be so simple—and boring. The mystery of life exists in its paradoxes and middle ground.

By avoiding extremes you have a greater chance of finding peace. However, in the upcoming paragraphs you will not find peace—only humor. I am sure you will recognize people you know or maybe parts of yourself in the following illusions.

What if you had to choose a belief by circling one of the three statements? In each case, which one would you pick?

1. Money is the answer to earthly happiness.
   Money was created by the devil.
   I am too spiritual or rich to be concerned about money.
2. Sex is the ultimate religious experience.
   Sex is evil.
   I am too pure or tired to be concerned with sex.
3. I should be overly attached to family and friends.
   I should not have contact with family and

friends.
I gave up family and friends long ago in my pursuit of God.

4. Power makes me supremely secure.
   Power leads to the downfall of man.
   I am too dumb or spiritual to be concerned with power.
5. Beauty makes me worthy of worship.
   Beauty is a curse.
   I have already transcended worldly concerns with beauty or have just won the Miss Universe contest (Mr. Universe contest for men) and do not want to think of beauty as an illusion.
6. Intelligence makes me superior.
   Intelligence makes me cruel or devoid of feeling.
   I am incapable of understanding the topic or am in a constant state of bliss and in perpetual contact with the universal intelligence.
7. Fame means people like me.
   Fame means people detest me.
   I had my quota of fame for this lifetime and am not concerned with the question, or I am beyond fame, or I am in jail (infamous, do not pass go, do not collect $200).
8. Success brings happiness.
   Success brings unhappiness.
   I am flowing in the here and now where success does not exist.

9. Love is rewarding.
   Love is unrewarding.
   I have attained the state of impersonal love where I remain stuck in the lotus position with little chance of rescue.

I hope you have enjoyed yourself as well as looked more deeply into the underlying messages of these examples. Too often you may have fenced yourself into a mental corner with an idea. Maybe it would be better to examine it with a humorous eye and let go of ideas that cannot laugh.

ABOUT THE AUTHOR

Terry Chitwood was born on November 10, 1947, in Milwaukee, Wisconsin. He graduated from high school at 17 and joined the service. During his tour of duty, he was in Guam, the Philippine Islands, Japan, and Vietnam. He graduated in 1972 from the University of Wisconsin (Milwaukee) magna cum laude with a B.A. in psychology. He received his M.A. in counseling psychology from the University of South Dakota in 1974. He graduated from the University of South Dakota in 1976 with an Ed.D. degree in counseling psychology.

Dr. Chitwood worked as a psychologist at Plains Area Mental Health Center, LeMars, Iowa; Redfield State Hospital, Redfield, South Dakota; West Iowa Mental Health Center, Carroll, Iowa; and the Ft. Grant Training Center (minimum security prison), Ft. Grant, Arizona. He developed the Polestar prison program at Ft. Grant where hardcore convicts were transformed into loving individuals. The program consisted of the following modalities: yoga, aikido, tai chi, rebirthing, postural restructuring, self-mastery, and a variety of psychological therapies. Dr. Chitwood is the founder of postural restructuring, a connective tissue and muscle manipulation system that releases bodily tension, relieves mental stress, and straightens the posture. He is also the founder of self-mastery, an effective method for spiritual development.

After making the prison program self-perpetuating, Dr. Chitwood started his own business in Phoenix called Polestar. He used the same modalities as in the prison program to help intelligent and self-aware individuals evolve their consciousness. Presently, he is working with his clients through Polestar in Sioux Falls, South Dakota, where he specializes in Jungian-oriented psychotherapy. Dr. Chitwood also conducts telephone sessions in which out-of-state individuals can work on their dreams and life problems.

ABOUT POLESTAR

If you enjoyed this book and desire more information about our other publications, tapes, sessions, and seminars, please contact us at the following address:

Polestar
620 South Minnesota
Sioux Falls, SD 57104